Ceremonial Confessions

Stories from a Church Organist

Andrew Whitenack

ANDDAR Publications

Cover photos: First Congregational United Church of Christ,
Pasadena, CA.

ISBN: 978-1-105-01737-7

Dedicated to Darin Stewart

Table of Contents

FOREWARD

Musicians are a special group of people. Whether you are a member of a rock band, string quartet, orchestra or even as a solitary church organist, you must master a multitude of skills and deal with many changing situations. Beginning as a youngster by learning your instrument, you labor and practice hours on end, attend lesson after lesson, becoming "one" with your instrument. Once confident enough with your abilities, you begin to share your skill with the community for fun and hopefully for profit.

Church musicians practice their craft weekly at rehearsals, worship services as well as many other events such as weddings and funerals. In Scott Francis Brenner's book *The Art of Worship* (Macmillan, 1961), he gives the church musician his guidelines on the music to be included in the marriage ceremony.

"The music agenda is apt to require considerable attention. Most people are ignorant concerning church music and those of us who know, or ought to know, must be patient and charitable. Nevertheless, some education, even though painful, is called for. We might begin by pointing to "Oh Promise Me," "I Love You Truly," "Because," "Ah! Sweet Mystery of Life" and the like as nonreligious sentimental pap, hardly the thing for mature folk. At the same time, we should be able to turn to the hymnal and suggest hymns fitting for all to sing...The instrumental music is equally difficult to handle. While Mendelssohn's and Wagner's wedding marches are deeply entrenched, surely the time is come when we must point out how inappropriate they are and take whatever reasonable steps are required to encourage their death knell."

As a church musician for over 30 years, spending 5 years on the east coast, 10 years on the mid-west and 15 years (so far) on the west coast, I have been employed by churches of three denominations. I have always been of the opinion that whatever music the bride wants played at her wedding, she should receive since her family is paying the bill. Consequently, I have played the traditional music and some sentimental pap myself throughout the years mixed with standard classical works. After playing for so many services, weddings and funerals throughout the years, a few of those services stand out from the rest as interesting, humorous and downright odd. Here is a collection of 14 humorous true stories for musicians, couples about to be married or anyone seeking a smile.

Andrew Whitenack

August, 2011

The Lord's Unknown

Some pieces of music are classics, known by all and enjoyed each and every time they are heard. Who can't help but enjoy Beethoven's Fifth Symphony, a Strauss Waltz or a lovely Mozart Sonata? Even with years of repetition, the listener and even the players never grow weary of these timeless pieces. The same can't be said for one of the most famously over-sung wedding solos of all time, *The Lord's Prayer* by Albert Hay Malotte. In Scott Francis Brenner's book *The Art of Worship* (Macmillan, 1961) he states that he hopes the minister "is in a position where he can suppress such other ill-conceived practices as the singing of *The Lord's Prayer…"*

A standard at many weddings, this schmaltzy war-horse is typically included while the bride and groom are enjoying a private moment together, kneeling at the altar in prayer. They usually have just finished lighting the single Unity Candle, signifying their hearts becoming one and are now contemplating the remaining minutes of the service along with their remaining years together. It may be that during this lengthy song, a single moment may surface and "forever" may seem like a "big mistake." Maybe during this song the first chip in the iceberg towards divorce occurs. And the vocalist pushes them, along with the audience, to that brink with stratospherically high notes while the accompanist pounds away on the repeating chords like hammering on a new roof. Grandiose and wickedly difficult!

I started learning this piece when I was a teenager for one of the first weddings I was hired to play. I spent hours laboring over the piece and particularly the last page of music, practicing over and over again like a stuck needle on an old album. The black notes on the page were oozing together into a river of mistakes as my fingers tried desperately to retain all of those flats, sharps and copious amounts of additional accidentals. "I know I'm going to mess up the climax...I just can't get it!" But, as fate was on my side this time, the piece went off okay, though there was a split-second pause or two while my memory regrouped the 5-note chords under my fingers. At least I don't remember the bride running out screaming, holding her ears. Nor do I recall any glaring mistakes or crashing wrong chords causing the audience to recoil in horror. The bride and her husband were divorced within a year anyway. Maybe she blames me for the separation.

As the years past, I was asked to play this piece countless times. Much to my dismay, each and every time it was requested, I had to pull out the correct version as there are several, in different keys and for different instruments-and basically relearn it again and again. My mind disliked the piece so much that my fingers refused to retain the music, much like blocking out a personal horrifying experience and then dredging it up and reliving it again. But after a few minutes of playing "that dreaded last page," the piece would finally come around and I would become master over it once more.

One of the recent times I played this piece was with a gentleman who, when I spoke to him on the phone, immediately relayed to me that he knew the piece well. Thinking there would be no need for any additional practice, we scheduled to rehearse together the day before the wedding. Arriving as planned, he was ready to get started. Odd, though, he didn't have any music with him so I quickly gave him an extra one of my copies and we began. After the few bars of keyboard introduction, he failed to enter on the first phrase. Thinking that he might just be nervous, we started again. At his entrance I nodded and mouthed the first couple of words and he started singing. Good. This is going fine. But as soon as I stopped mouthing the words, he stopped singing again. Uh-Oh. This doesn't look good. I see danger ahead. When I stopped and asked him if everything was ok, was I playing too fast or too slow he smiled and said no but he didn't read music and had never *sung* the song before. I reminded him of his previous comment and he said yes, that he *knew of* the song but had never actually performed it. Ding-ding-ding. The red warning light in my head is flashing. Now what do we do? He said he could follow me if I continued to mouth the words for him. So we started once more, this time I mouthed the words as much as I could and we got through the whole piece. There were skips and jumps throughout the rhythm but I followed him. After several more times through, I told him I thought it would be fine as long as he did it exactly the same way at the wedding. The next day, in order to accomplish this masquerade, I turned the 7ft grand piano so my back was toward the audience and I was directly facing Mr. Vocalist. All he had to do was look down from the podium and follow me. I don't like this much responsibility but at this point there was little else I could do.

When it was time for him to sing, we worked together and miraculously, the solo actually came off ok, with only an occasional jump across some music on my part to catch up with him, and it sounded presentable. By this point in my career I thought I was ready for anything but not for a quasi-vocalist/friend-of-the-bride who had never sung the selected song before. Make sure your soloist is really a soloist and not just using your wedding ceremony as a practice run for an American Idol audition.

Bless Their Hearts!

Living in the mid-west before moving to Los Angeles, I learned what the term *rural* really meant. I lived near the capital of the state myself but less than an hour away from the city there were old farm houses badly in need of paint, collapsed barns, rusted abandoned plows, and little white churches. On occasion, there were even farmers riding horses alongside of your car on those back country roads where willows border and branches weep low into your lane. A potential cover of the *Saturday Evening Post* around each bend.

A friend of mine from graduate school was asked to sing at one of his relatives weddings. The service was to be small and being held way out in the back woods country and in one of those little white churches. Jeff was asked to sing one song during the lighting of the Unity Candle. In the weeks preceding the ceremony, we met together and rehearsed his song a number of times in order to have a perfect presentation the day of the wedding. At the beginning when he first asked me to accompany him, I asked about the music for the rest of the service. "You don't have to worry about that. They already have someone to play for the rest of the service. I am just singing the solo." Perfect. This would be an extremely easy performance, or so I thought. Jeff then commented "and they don't have much money so I told them you would probably play for free. I hope that's okay with you." Well, it wasn't but I was already committed.

Since the church was several miles away from the area where I lived, Jeff and I rode through the countryside together. Arriving to a small, octagonal shaped church on the side of a dirt road, we went inside. The interior was complete with hard wooden benches to keep the congregants awake, a small wooden altar and a modest pulpit at the front. Shades on the windows to pull down if the sun became oppressive and two hanging pendent lights on long chains to brighten those long, evening revival meetings. Over to one side was a small spinet piano.

A few guests had already begun to arrive as two women decorated the altar with modest flowers of marigolds and phlox. We headed to the front of the room and took our seats near the piano. Over the next half hour, the room began to fill with family and friends. My soloist friend Jeff had been circulating around the room, chatting with some of his relatives, the wedding party and various guests, waiting for the service to begin. Suddenly, at 1:45, he returned to his seat next to mine and announced that the scheduled pianist was not going to be able to make it and he told the bride and groom that I would be happy to fill in since we were already there. I was stunned! Volunteering me without even asking and me without any music!

Not wanting the service to be a flop with no music, I reluctantly said "ok" and grabbed the nearest hymnal from the pew. The whole service consisted of hymns for the Prelude, a hymn for the Processional and hymns for the Recessional along with the special rehearsed solo that

Jeff sang. You certainly couldn't have attended a more "sacred" wedding and in the end, the music probably fit into the stodgy and conservative gathering better than other selections I might have played. "<u>Bless your heart</u> for filling in at the last minute. We sure do appreciate it" came a reply from one guest. Even today, I still wonder if they ever really had another pianist lined up in the first place or had Jeff planned this surprise ending from the very beginning with his family. I didn't receive any payment for the service. Either way, that day I learned to always carry an abundance of extra wedding music in my car at all times. So tomorrow, I am only *attending* a funeral of a friend but if the musician fails to show up, during the ceremony, you might hear me playing *We've Only Just Begun.*

Combination Day

Designated Holidays alone can be fun and relaxing, especially the single Holidays. President's Day, Valentine's Day, Memorial Day and the rest have a unique charm as a small respite or mini-vacation during an otherwise mechanical week. Especially rewarding is the single day off from work, usually filled with plans for all sorts of good intentions that are rarely completed or perhaps even started. When the day off falls on a Monday, therein lies a recovery day for many of those who have over indulged in whatever vice took hold of them on Friday evening. For the rest of us, we see what follows the Monday off as a short work week. Yes, we have just had a wonderful three day weekend but look what we have now! Only a four day work week. As a musician, keeping holidays and special events separate works best. Enjoy the holiday as intended and don't mix and match your events. This was never more evident to me as when I received a call to play piano at a local restaurant for an upcoming wedding.

In my hometown, there is a beautiful Colonial mansion with a nice piece of land surrounding the majestic brick structure. Tall white columns stretched up across the front, supporting a sizeable porch. Black shutters accented the stately home's many windows. Several years ago, the estate was sold and remodeled into an up-scale restaurant called *Le Manoir Colonial.* So elegant, so expensive and so *French.*

I spoke to Michelle briefly on the phone. She was so excited because her wedding was fast approaching. As with many young brides, the event itself is the most important thing and the music is secondary. All the better for me as this meant I would have to spend only a minimum amount of time preparing. "Just play whatever you like. I'm sure it will be fine" she chirped. "I want that regular piece for my entrance and we have a recording for the recessional" Excellent choices! Even easier. This will be a breeze. I'll play whatever I want, send her down the "isle" or whatever might be designated as her runway and be out of there quick with the cash. Perhaps she will saunter past the buffet table before arriving in front of the minister. The Unity Candle may be placed on the bar "just for the effect" as a guest might later recount. "And what's the date?" I asked. "It's at 1:00 pm on Mother's Day" she cheerfully replied. "It will be held outdoors, at the side of the restaurant, off of the side porch." Well, I guess this won't be too bad although restaurants are notorious for being crowded on Mother's Day. And where will the piano be located? Outside in the hot sun?

After playing for my regular church job in the morning, I raced across town and arrived at *Le Manoir Colonial* in plenty of time. The large side parking lot was full but after circling once around the whole lot, I was able to find a spot near to the last exit at the back edge. This must be a bigger wedding than I initially thought. I hope they have room for the guests seated outside. Carrying my music, I entered the large estate front door. The maître d' welcomed me and showed me the piano. There, right inside the main front door, in the center of the front foyer was a suitable, small baby grand. Standing around in the foyer with us were small groups of people waiting for a table to have Mother's Day lunch. The tables were all filled with lovely families, dressed up for the occasion, and mother's seated proudly as the centerpiece of the day. Finally, the wedding coordinator arrived and explained the details of the procession to me. It seems that while I would be here, seated at the piano, just inside the main entrance, the entire wedding would be taking place completely outside on the north area of the lawn. Someone standing with the wedding party would signal the next person who would be standing at the side door entrance of the mansion who would then signal the coordinator standing across the foyer who would then signal me. Then I would begin playing the procession music. When signaled again, it would be time for me to quickly switch music and play the Bride's March. The piano has been equipped with a microphone to pipe the music to the outside audience through speakers. Well, I do wish the piano was closer so I could at least see *something* of the wedding but that's not going to happen. All right, I think I can handle this.

At 12:30, I begin prelude music. I am calm and enjoying the surroundings and the people are enjoying the music. Maybe this won't be so bad after all. As I continue playing, more families have exited their respective religious establishments from around town and descended on the restaurant. More and more people are coming in and the foyer is quickly getting full. People are talking louder now and stacking up around me. There is nowhere for them to sit. Soon, I feel like a turkey at Thanksgiving just arriving at the table fresh out of the oven. There is now a complete circle of people around me, at the edges of the piano, all staring down at me.

Luckily, it is soon to be over. I see the coordinator's cue for the procession to begin. Keeping an eye on her and one also my music, she signals again for the Bride's March. As she gives me the "cut" sign, I know the wedding party is in place and the minister can take over. I am sweating bullets but finally my part of the ceremony is complete. The nightmare is over. I receive a round of applause for the patron's waiting for their luscious Mother's Day lunch. I acknowledge them but quickly gather my belongings and head for the door.

I never met or saw the bride or anyone from the entire wedding party or any of the family or guests. The coordinator gave me my money. It was the most 'remote' wedding I was ever involved with. So if you are planning a wedding, do yourself and your musicians a favor and pick your own date just for you and your spouse that isn't already a recognized holiday and leave the combos at the fast food restaurant.

Hee Haw

Friends are wonderful things. They can lift your spirits and help you through a rough time in your life. They can be an ally in those confrontational times when two are better than one. They can also cause you embarrassment just for being their friend.

Early in my wedding career, I was asked by a high school friend named Mary if I would play for her wedding. It was going to be very small and even at the same church where I was currently accompanying the youth choir. Being 17 or 18 years old, I could always use the extra money. She was a couple of years older than me but still way too young to be getting married. I agreed to play for her anyway. Now, some 38 years later, I can't remember much about the service at all except a couple of glaring points. The music was fine and there were no surprises. The wedding party itself was another story.

There were absolutely no guests. In this giant empty Sanctuary easily able to seat 1000 people, the whole wedding party consisted of the Minister, Bride, Groom, Best Man and the Maid of Honor. The bride wore a nice wedding veil along with her regular street clothes. I seem to remember that they were blue jeans but at least clean and nice looking and nothing particularly nice or expensive. Mary wasn't the kind to wear a dress on any occasion, either at church or school.

She was in the band and the band uniform pants suited her just fine. I always thought of her as a tomboy. Why should the wedding be any different? As we continued, the service followed the regular Christian order and she did have the traditional "Processional" down the middle aisle. Everything was going as planned and progressing as a regular wedding except for the empty pews. But even in all of this, the most unusual aspect of the whole service came when the bride began to speak her vows.

After the minister read them softly, Mary began to repeat them into the microphone. At that instant, she began to giggle. Softly at first, under her breath but loud enough to be heard. With each additional repeated phrase, the giggling grew louder and stronger until she was in full laughing mode. Stopping to catch her breath, she backed away from the mic and looked down at the floor. Her shoulders heaved as she tried in vain to hold in the noise. But it was too late. Now the minister had joined her as well. Next came the groom but not to the same extent as the rest. I, myself was mortified. I had never seen this type of display and I couldn't imagine such a thing even happening during a sacred, solemn occasion. Then I immediately remembered a similar situation with a different Mary. *The Mary Tyler Moore Show* had an episode in which the whole staff was attending the funeral of their friend Chuckles the Clown. As the Minister was giving the eulogy, Mary starts to giggle, quickly followed by uncontrolled laughter, but in the end, finally loudly sobbing in sorrow at the death of a friend. I giggled a little myself wondering if this service would have the same ending. After regaining composure, the service continued without incident. In the end, it was probably to her advantage that no guests were there to witness the spectacle.

I haven't kept in touch with Mary over these many years but I have seen her recently on a social network site through other close friends. She appears to still be married but I can't remember her first married name from long ago so who knows. Maybe this is husband number three and maybe over the years, Mary has giggled her way through a couple spousal funerals of her own too.

Merry Rentmas

When I first moved to California in the late 90's, I was looking for any number of ways to pay the rent. Professional musicians or musicians who try to make a living and survive on just a music career learn to work within the system and spend much of their time doing a variety of music-related jobs to earn income. I was no different. I was playing every week at a local church, directing the choirs, teaching at a music conservatory part-time, working with a piano restoration company during the day and doing a few outside piano tunings when the schedule permitted. Believe it or not, I was able to get all of these duties accomplished. The schedule was hectic, yes, but with such a variety of jobs who could get bored? There wasn't time for it! I was learning to maneuver my way around the wonderful city of Los Angeles. Throwing a tuning in here or a wedding in there wasn't too bad as long as I was careful and didn't overbook.

At that time in my music career, the church that had recently employed me had a temporary interim minister. We got along fine because I didn't question her authority since I was new but not everyone saw rainbows and sunshine above her head. Her job was to shake things up and try and reunite the congregation in a new vision towards the future and incorporate new ideas. I benefited only once from one of her changes. I call it *"Divine Intervention."*

After only being employed with the church for a couple of months, this minister decided that she, myself and the wedding coordinators were not being paid enough for our wedding services. Of course, not wanting to make waves, I totally agreed with her. She raised my compensation by almost an additional $100 per wedding. Yippee! I can always use more money, starving musician still, trying to get by. The building manager at the time was the person who scheduled all of the weddings taking place throughout the year. Usually, there are less than 20 per year so picking a vacant date was never a problem for the bride. This particular Saturday in June, however, two weddings had been scheduled for the same day. Luckily, the Building Manager that placed each on the schedule left a couple of hours in between in order to clear everyone out, clean up, and then redecorate for the next wedding. Putting them on my schedule a few weeks in advance, I decided that this would be fine. I could easily make this work.

As the Saturday drew closer, there was suddenly an event in downtown Los Angeles that needed a piano tuned. There was a special event being held outside and in front of a famous high-end auction house. The piano would be dropped off, literally on the curb early in the morning, the guy said. I told him I would do it. Then within a day or two, I received another tuning job for early the same evening. I began to wonder how versatile I could be in one day. Can I race around and get all of this completed without falling flat on my face? Sure, why not? So I said yes to that tuning as well. Yes to everything!

On that day, I hurried to downtown just as the sun was coming up on another beautiful Southern California day. I arrived just as the piano was delivered. Hurrying through the tuning, I finished and headed for wedding number one. Got through that one, had lunch, went back and played for the second wedding then off to the last tuning. When I made it home, I was exhausted. Nothing spectacular or bizarre happened that day but I had made enough money in that one day to pay a whole month's rent with some extra on top. I was happy. I was very happy because Christmas was just around the corner. Unfortunately the happiness was short lived. After only one more wedding, the church governing committee decided that they didn't like the higher prices. They overrode the minister's increases and lowered everyone's compensation back to our original amount. Then, within six months, the interim minister abruptly resigned during one of her worship services, never to return. I also called that *"Divine Intervention."*

Larghetto in Es

Hey Judee

After grad school in the mid 80's, I was living in a very small town in the mid-west. Some of the first weddings that I performed at as a professional musician were while I was living here. A testing ground, as it were, for the many years to follow in CA. At that time, I was organist at a tiny country Lutheran church. The Sunday services followed the traditional Lutheran Liturgy, incorporating the style of the mass with cantor singing and congregational responses. On most Sundays, the minister strictly followed the regular service as provided from the Lutheran Book of Worship. But we were also a mildly liberal church as well, tending to vary the services a little to make them more interesting. Some Sundays, the minister decided to just read the chants instead of singing them but the congregation and myself always responded in song. This is what they were used to. It was their tradition. Before I arrived, they had always sung the same setting of liturgical music, Sunday after Sunday, for several years, following the same old tradition and procedure. After being there for several years, I convinced them to at least learn an alternate version of the music. After they learned a different setting, we switched back and forth depending on the church season. I taught them that a little variety was a good thing.

One day, I was approached by a senior citizen member of my choir.

She asked me if I could play for her sons' second wedding. I agreed and she then told me that the bride wanted an "all Beatles Wedding." Stunned, I asked her if she was mistaken and didn't she mean all Beatles reception? Naturally, it would make more sense since the bride and groom were both in their mid 30's and would have been teens during the Beatles era. They could dance the night away to all of their old favorites. But, no, she actually meant for the wedding itself. All Beatles music from beginning to end.

Having just recently finished graduate school and received my Master's Degree, I was still riding high on the scholarliness of Beethoven, Bach and Brahms. How could anyone want such "pop fluff" for their solemn, sacred occasion? This wasn't Las Vegas. These were solid Evangelical Lutherans. But being the obedient musician, I pulled together what was requested.

The day of the wedding included Prelude music of "And I Love Her", "The Long and Winding Road", and "I Want to Hold Your Hand." The bride processed in to "Yesterday" and the Unity Candle was lit during a meditative and reflective "Hey Jude." Finally, as if to add a last jab to the traditional Lutheran wedding service, the party recessed out of the church to "Why Don't We Do It in the Road?" All in all, a lovely final selection for the guests to hum as they head off to the reception. I didn't attend so I never knew how far the "all Beatles" theme was actually carried.

For the rest of my long wedding career when I was discussing music with a bride-to-be there were usually questions about certain songs. One particular bride asked "Is it okay for you to play 'My Heart Will Go On' the theme from Titanic in a church?" My reply was "Hey Judee, You are the bride and I will play whatever you would like. You know, once upon a time there was an all Beatles wedding…"

Maybe Later

I am always on time. In fact, I am always early. I'm the guy who gets the first parking space at a show. I like being the first in line at the ticket counter. When I was a smoker, this was my chance to have one last cigarette before entering a smoking-banned area and I knew it might be a few hours before I could light up again and escape into that wonderful haze of my own personal chimney. But I also don't want to miss anything that I am attending. I don't want to be that person walking in late and stepping on someone's foot or ending up standing in the back stretching to see whatever wonder is unfolding up front, out of my sight range.

There are any number of reasons why the rest of the world is late and I'm sure many are actually good reasons. The car broke down. There was an accident. Someone was sick at the last minute. Someone died. Whatever the reason, I don't like being that late person. I have eight watches so that on any given morning, if the battery of one has died overnight, at least I have several others to choose from along with the clock on my phone and in my car. I don't really care why others are late. I am always on time.

For several years at my current church position, I had a whole wedding music routine worked out in my head. The service always played out correctly but not without some minor adjustments. I would plan out everything that I was going to play for a wedding, write down a general length in minutes and be ready to finish up my music just as the wedding was about to start. I used to pride myself in how close I could work it out, depending on how big the wedding turned out to be or how fussy the bride was or how much time pre-wedding pictures took. Sometimes it worked perfectly, many times it didn't. More times than not, I would have to scramble at the last minute and toss in a couple of church hymns to extend the time while feverishly watching the door for the cue that everyone was in place at the back and ready for the processional. Hasn't everyone hummed along softly while the organist plays *Joy to the World* at the last wedding they attended?

At this afternoon wedding, I could tell by the casual attitude of everyone that my perfect system wasn't going to work this time. So I gathered a couple of extra pieces just in case I needed to play for another 5 minutes or so. The wedding was at 2:00 PM. I began playing nice soothing background music at 1:35. These things always run late so I don't start to get worried until 30-35 minutes have passed. The Chapel is almost full and people are chatting quietly as they usually do during the prelude. At 2:15, the wedding coordinator slipped up to the organ and whispered in my ear. "The minister isn't here yet and the bride's not quite ready. They would like you to play for a few more minutes." Fine. I can do that for a few more minutes. I start repeating the pieces I have already played using different registrations to at least make them *seem* different. The audience is beginning to talk louder.

At about 2:40, now an hour has passed from when I began. As I continue, I see the coordinator approaching me once again. "The minister is here but the bride isn't quite ready yet. They would like you to continue to play for a few more minutes." I tell the coordinator, while I continue to play, that I am all out of music and I have been playing an hour already and I will have to just play some hymns. She agrees and leaves again. I frantically begin taxing my ability and start sight-reading through some of the songs in my wedding book that I haven't even ever looked at before. I discovered that if you play something slow enough, you can actually hit all of the correct notes! At this point, several people in the audience have left their seats, and are moving around the room, shaking hands and chatting with the other guests. Some of the more boisterous patrons are getting really loud, laughing and having a good time.

Finally, it's now 2:55 and once again I see the coordinator coming up the isle towards me. This time she is bound to say that we are ready to begin. Alas, I hear the same words again for a 3rd time. "The bride isn't quite ready and they would like you to play for a few more minutes." It was at this point I turned to her and abruptly said "No." As soon as the song I was playing ended, so did I. I stopped playing and the audience instantly hushed to a soft murmur. People took their seats but continued to chat. I looked through the wedding program and checked under my fingernails for dirt. I dusted off the edges of the keyboard. I straightened up my music. After about fifteen minutes, the bride finally appeared and the wedding began. It was a short ceremony so I wasn't there too long anyway.

After that day, I never again played any extra music. If the wedding party isn't ready and has held up the service and all of the guests more than 10-15 minutes, I've done enough. I simply stop playing. It's not my fault. I'm always on time.

Fainting Sam

Stage fright is a fact of life. Those performers that say they don't experience any stage fright are unbelievably secure or lying. From the time I was about 12 years old, playing the piano in public always frightened me. It is amazing that I have ended up doing as much performing as I do given the stage fright that I experience. And with age comes even more insecurity. When I was in college, I practiced enough to get by. I had some stage fright at recital times and jury days but it wasn't enough to prompt me to practice more and try to eliminate the feelings completely. On one occasion when I was particularly underprepared, I jumped up out of my seat from the recital audience and headed for a practice room in the building to quickly practice the opening section of the piece I was about to perform. While sitting there, I couldn't remember how the piece even started! Luckily, I regained the piece and played at my appointed time in the recital. Besides being nervous with sweating and shaky hands, I have been able to manage my stage fright pretty well.

Weddings are always nerve racking mostly because of timing issues. Will the bride fall while walking down the aisle? Will the tiny 2 year old ring bearer child suddenly burst into tears and head for its mother, leaving a gap to be filled with music? The actual playing usually happens easily because I have a set number of songs in my repertoire that I rotate over and over again with different weddings. The most stage fright I ever have is when the bride is processing down the isle. No one wants to hit a single wrong note and spoil an otherwise beautiful procession. And with today's recording capabilities, your glaring mistake will be captured for all eternity. I can happily say that in my entire career of playing for weddings, I have never made a glaring mistake during the bride's entrance. Now for other performances, I practice the pieces to death to make sure I know them as well as I possibly can.

In my youth, my playing career began with accompanying the youth choir at my church. I was only 14 years old when I began learning teen cantatas and swinging Baptist musicals. I would get nervous before the actual performance but during the singing, I enjoyed playing. I can't say the same for my friend, Sam who sang in the choir. He had a nice voice and on this particular occasion, he had been given a brief solo. Rehearsals went fine and so did the actual performance. Once Sam finished singing he part, he stepped back into the group and we continued the musical together. A minute later, Sam fell straight back, knees locked, flat on his back with a thud. Everyone stopped singing but I was positioned at the piano to the side and off of the stage area so I didn't see exactly what had happened. I only heard a muffled "thud." I continued on playing until I saw the conductor giving me the "cut, cut" sign. Finally, I stopped. Several people from the audience jumped up and ran up to Sam. As soon as they bent his knees up, he regained consciousness. He stood up, the helpers retreated back to the audience and the choir reassembled. Now I am so involved with watching the group that I am not paying attention to the director. He is glaring at me and waving his arms frantically, trying to get my attention. Suddenly, I see that he is beating time and wants me to start playing and finally, I return to the music and the choir took off singing again. The rest of the performance was uneventful.

That day I learned that you never lock your knees while standing for a long time, especially if you are prone to extreme stage fright.... or fainting.

Odd Couple

All of us have heard of the old saying about couples that are married for a long time start to look like each other. We have even see pictures to support this theory. I have received fun "pass-it-on" emails depicting elderly couples, after having been married for 30, 40 or 50 years, with obvious facial similarities and looking more like siblings than partners. Amazing and uncanny, right?

In 2005, I played for a wedding that will obviously not have the look-a-like ending that people enjoy seeing. There was nothing special about the music selections, they opted for me to choose and play whatever I would like. To me, these were my favorite weddings. They required the smallest amount of work on my part and the least amount of practice and preparation. Sometimes, I am just lazy. I would just play all of my regular pieces.

When the evening of the rehearsal arrived, I was already at the church when the couple came into the chapel together. The groom was a wonderful man. In appearance, he was a short, stocky, bald, very dark Jamaican man with a great personality and a large smile. He agreed to do whatever his soon-to-be bride wanted that would make her happy. She was also a lovely lady. She was very tall, thin, and pale skinned with platinum blonde hair looking much like a native Swedish woman. She was also very happy to be getting married the next day. The couple was glowing and much in love.

I learned that the bride was actually from Kentucky after speaking to her parents as they arrived a few minutes later for the rehearsal. They were quiet, reserved people and they were keeping their distance. The thin father was dressed in classic bibbed overalls and a flannel shirt. The mother, who was slightly overweight, slowly made her way into the pew. Following close behind was the even larger younger sister. She had some of the same traits as her older sister but obviously a product of the TV/video game generation. She quickly sat down and remained there until everything was finished like a piece of gum on your shoe.

After a short time, the groom's family arrived. All of them were native Jamaican's complete with the beautiful accents, fetching smiles and gregarious mannerisms. Following brief introductions, the two families separated into the two different sides of the room. The rehearsal continued without a hitch.

The next day at the wedding, the scene from the previous evening was repeated again but now, on a much larger scale. The bride's Kentuckian family and friends filled up one side of the Chapel and the groom's Jamaican family and friends filled up the other. The Kentuckians were all dressed in their Sunday-Go-To-Meeting outfits but the Jamaicans outdid everyone. The immediate family and even some of the friends came dressed in their native Jamaican outfits, complete with the beautiful bright print fabrics, flowing robes, jewelry and tall fancy hats. I have never seen such polar opposites together in one place. It was quite amazing. When the minister said "You may kiss the bride" what he actually meant was "You may now bend down and kiss the groom." As the service ended and I watched this bride, two feet taller than her groom, recess out together, I realized again that true happiness might actually be found in that little space of differences between two people.

Sci-Fi Bible School Convention

Growing up in a smaller town meant that opportunities for making money as a musician were limited to whatever you could get either by referrals or word of mouth. Musicians must say "yes" to as many jobs as possible in order to pay the rent. Whenever two or more jobs fall on the same date either by accident or because of a desperate need of cash, the player must figure out how to wear two hats at the same time.

During the time right after college, I took a job as an accompanist for a professional singer in my hometown. She was a professional as one could be in a small town of 100,000. She had a whole stage persona and she loved performing. I frequently accompanied her at dinners, openings, festival weekends and the like. Sometimes she was just one of the acts and other times, she was running the whole show. We had fun together but since I was busy with a part-time and full -time job and she had a family, we didn't get to practice enough together to make a great duo.

In June of that year, whatever year that was in the mid-1980's, Susan had been elected chairman of a valley-wide science-fiction convention. Laura Banks from Star Trek II was the special guest and it was a big deal to the area sci-fi fans. The dinner at the convention hotel was on a Friday night and it was formal. I loved these events. Since I had yet to be away from my hometown, I felt like I was in the big time. Fancy clothes, fancy dinner, and dim mood lighting. Susan had scheduled herself to sing a program of songs before the actual dinner and she planned to sing a few more after the dinner hour, followed by a brief program. Just like a Hollywood premier! But next came my scheduling conflict. At the church where I was currently employed, Vacation Bible School was wrapping up a weeklong of sacred festivities that same Friday night and there was a large commencement program planned. Children were going to sing and present their tempera painted macaroni pictures of Jesus to their parents. Since it was my regular paying job, I was required to be there and play for the little children as they processed into the church for their vocal program. But needing the money, I decided to try to squeeze both events into the same evening. I could do it. I knew I could.

I started out my evening at the posh hotel, dressed in black tux pants, white tux coat, tux shirt and red bowtie. Everyone was enjoying cocktails standing around elegantly clothed tables. The entertainment portion began and Susan and I presented a medley of current pop, crowd-pleasing hits. The second that Susan finished singing her first program and the dinner portion began, I dashed to the car, sped across town to the church and arrived only minutes before the service was to begin. Taking deep breaths and entering into the Sanctuary, I was terribly overdressed with all of the little children, parents and teachers in shorts and sandals on this hot summer evening. The program went fine, I played perfect and the kids had a fun time but the second the program was over, I closed the piano and ran out to my car, headed back across town to the hotel to arrive just as dinner had finished and they were introducing the special guests. After sitting for a few minutes and gathering my wits again, Susan was up to sing and we finished up a couple last songs. I circled around the room and got some autographs from people I don't know and have never heard of again and then left.

I made some good money that night at the convention dinner but I was reprimanded the following week by the stodgy minister at the church. He was unhappy that I didn't stay around at the end of the service and socialize with people and told me that it looked bad that I was running out of the building so quickly once the service was over. He also used that time to go over some things about my job performance that he wasn't happy with, telling me he was the leader of the team and that if I wasn't on board with following the leader of the team that I needed to get off the team. And that's just what I did. One month later I resigned to go back to college in the mid-west to get my master's degree and ultimately play for many services and weddings and programs throughout my remaining career. But never again did I ever play for a Bible School program or two events on the same night.

Language Fence

Living in Los Angeles one quickly adapts to the many diverse cultures and nationalities that exist throughout the vast metropolitan area. Some think this diversity as a bother and would prefer to live completely with their own kind. Others find living amongst a broad spectrum of peoples a wonderfully stimulating life, often embracing other cultural traditions and practices. My own church congregation is a perfect example. The Walker's immediately come to mind. Mr. Walker is Protestant and Mrs. Walker is Jewish. Even though we are a Protestant church, she is a faithful member of my choir and participates in all aspects of the traditional Christian service. But once a year, she plans and executes a Jewish Seder meal for anyone who would like to experience a tradition from another religion. I attend because I love the horoset and the wine.

Having moved from the mid-west, it took me a while to grow accustomed to this diversity but as time went on, everyone blended together to form the cultural melting pot that is Los Angeles. My own experience, though not particularly earth shattering, was interesting to me.

The area I live in has a large, young Asian population, many attending college nearby. Though my own congregation includes only a few members of Asian decent, the area around the church is home to many lovely Asian people. Since our building is used for anyone who wishes to rent the space, I have played for a large number of Asian weddings over the past 15 years. The service is basically the same but hearing it performed in another language is fascinating. Oh, there are variations of the candle lighting, kneeling prayer, greeting of parents, etc., but the order is the same. The immediate families come robed in their own beautiful traditional garb, complete with fabrics flowing to the ground and maximum embroidery.

In these wedding services, there was always a Minister who spoke the native language, be it Japanese, Chinese or Korean and a second, translative Minister to repeat everything in English. It was just like sub-titles in a foreign movie without actually having to read them. As organist, I received my musical queues from the English speaker. But finally, there was one Korean wedding without the English translations.

At the rehearsal, there was very little English spoken and I had difficulty following where we were in the service. Finally, when it was all over, I tried to speak to the Minister who barely understood my English. "How will I know when you are ready for me to play the Processional?" He nodded politely, repeatedly and said "Yes, every-thing won-der-ful. Service tomorrow okay. Bye-bye." And with that, he was gone, headed out with the rest of the group. What will I do tomorrow?

When the service time arrived the next day, I began playing as usual. Only 15 minutes into my Prelude music, out pops the minister with the groomsmen, ready to begin the service. Yikes! Quickly I resolved that chord, finished that phrase and got ready for the Processional. From across the room, he looked at me, smiled and nodded so I began to play the wedding party music. In came the bridesmaids, groomsmen, flower girls and parents. As I stopped to prepare for the bride, the minister who was still across the altar, turned and in his loud broken English voice exclaimed "Pro-ces-sion-al!" That's my queue. In came the bride. Once at the front, the Korean service started. Listening intently and not knowing what I was hearing, suddenly the minister turned again to me, shouting "Hymn!" I played the chosen hymn and the whole congregation of over 500 people stood and began singing in Korean. It was a sound like I had never heard before. Music so familiar to me but unknown words. When we finished, he seated the congregation and proceeded with the lengthy service. There was a very long 20-25 minute sermon somewhere in the middle. After a couple of minutes past the hymn, I pulled out my book and began to read because I knew this was going to be a long one.

Finally, when I sensed the end was near, I prepared the last music. The Minister was praying softly, holding his hand over the kneeling couple and the rest of the congregation bowing in prayer. After a minute or two, the Minister abruptly turned once again and loudly proclaimed "Re-ces-sion-al" emphasizing each syllable. I played and out they all marched. The whole service was over and there was no translation. I didn't understand any of it except for my three queue words. But then again, I knew that it didn't matter to me and that the couple was in love and that's all that mattered to everyone else. The language fence became a bridge for me to cross over, briefly, into another culture.

Ready, Set, Go

Occasionally, there is a request to play for a wedding that is being held somewhere other than your own church. Along with that request come all sorts of wonderful "unknowns." Where is it located? What type of instrument will be available? How terrible will it sound? At least in my own building I am familiar with the sound, the space, the instruments and, most important of all, the procedure. There is great comfort and peace that at least my part will be completed smooth and fluently. The wedding coordinator and I have the whole service down to a science with specific cues having exact meanings. As long as a photographer doesn't get in the way and block my view, the whole processional and recessional of the entire wedding party always runs smoothly. The guests sit back and enjoy a perfectly timed procession with the bride stopping at the waiting arm of her soon-to-be husband just as I finish playing her brilliant wedding march. Whatever happens once the couple has ended the long walk to the altar is up to the minister at that point. If the bride faints or her veil catches on fire at the Unity Candle, well, that's not my problem. And finally at the end of the service, I take over once more to send the whole group off to the happy reception.

I received a phone call to play for a wedding at a church in a nearby town. They told me that the church doesn't use the organ and there wasn't anyone to play and she really wanted organ during her service. I agreed and asked her for the particulars like rehearsal time, wedding time, etc. When I looked on the map, I noticed that a large wholesale club in which I was a member of was nearby so I took a friend with me so we could check it out after the rehearsal.

When I arrived at the small church, I began to search for the organ. After searching around in the usual places at the front of the sanctuary with no luck, I was told that it was located in the balcony which, of course, was locked and no one was there to unlock the door. Eventually, by the time the family got there, I was able to locate someone to open the door. After climbing up the narrow balcony steps, I found the organ. It was more like a piece of old discarded furniture. It was covered with dirt and dust and had books piled on it. It was even painted blue. I was told that they don't use it anymore but it still *might* work. I turned it on, tried to clean it up as best I could so I could play. A few keys were broken but for the most part, it did still work. The console was built in and I sat facing the back of the building. There was no mirror or anyway to see what was going on in the main sanctuary below. How on earth could I pull this off? I got off the bench, walked down and looked over the balcony and saw the family was all assembled below. Since I had a friend with me sitting in the audience, I motioned for him to come up. I asked him to sit at the edge of the balcony and watch the ceremony during the rehearsal and tell me what was happening so I knew when to play the processional, the bride's entrance and the recessional at the end. Ready? Set? Ok…go!

After the rehearsal, I went downstairs and talked to the family. They were very nice and even handed me my check with payment in full. The groom kidded with me that I still needed to come back the next day and play the service. This was the only time I was ever paid *before* the actual wedding. What happens if I happen to be sick tomorrow or have an accident on the way home that would prevent me from showing up the next day?

Happily, I was not sick and I did return the next day. I arrived early so I could be better prepared by practicing the prelude music and testing the different registrations. Now the listener will be able to hear a variety of sounds and songs while preparing for the ultimate service. But as I arrived at the door, there was a wedding already in progress. The church building people told me that they run weddings in this sanctuary all day long, every Saturday, scheduled 1 ½ hours apart. I can go in as soon as this one is finished. So I waited and eventually got in shortly before it was time to begin. No time for nice registrations. No time for practice on this close-and-play organ. I set up the registrations on the organ and started the prelude music. Once finished, I checked over the balcony and played the processional. Sitting at the balcony edge, I watched the service and finished with the recessional. Everything went off without a problem but the whole service was nerve racking just the same.

As I was exiting the building, the next wedding group was waiting outside to take our places. I don't know what instruments were normally used for these weekly Saturday Wedding Marathons but that's one poor organ that finished its race years ago and should stay in retirement.

Agitation & Nauseation

Weddings are not the only stressful services an organist may be asked to endure. Sometime length is a problem. Southern Baptist services can drag on and on while the organist and congregation continue to hum softly just one more verse of *Just As I Am*. Perhaps that lost soul that hasn't yet stepped forward during the previous eight verses will finally come forward to be received into the fellowship of the church. Or maybe that soul comes forward just so the song will finally be over. Then there is the Minister that continues preaching, seemingly oblivious to the time. While the organist reads the bulletin, some older members begin to nod off. I have even caught a glimpse of one of my choir members checking the inside of an eyelid or two. After 25 minutes, Mrs. Bannister, sitting in her regular spot on the front row, keeps checking her watch, raising her arm high enough in front of her face to try and catch the attention of the preacher. A little cough added to emphasize her impatience. Occasionally though, a regular Sunday morning worship service can have some added drama and excitement quite by accident and it can be something to talk about for the next few months as well.

On one particular occasion, a small group of special needs adults were sitting on the first row of the Chapel. Usually very well mannered and a wonderful addition to our congregation, this particular Sunday one of the young ladies was agitated by some outside event that happened before arriving at the service. As the choir sang their special anthem, she appeared to become more agitated with the crescendos of the music.

Soon the choir and congregation were clapping and joining in with the festive swinging beat of the gospel music. Everyone was having a great time. Finally, the piece ended on a particularly loud and extended "Yeahhhhhhhhhh" while I played gospel-style rocking chords in both hands and a *fff* glissando down the keyboard.

As soon as the song stopped and there was silence, this young lady stood up, slammed both hands down on the pew in front of her and yelled in a loud voice $#@%!!!!! (you may insert the expletive beginning with F and ending with K here) The music had been too much for her to handle and she had to "let it out!" Quickly, an adult came to her side and helped her out of the service. As of yet, for disrupting the service, she hasn't been allowed to return.

Within a year or so, another incident involving a different special needs adult occurred. Our main Sanctuary is built in the old Gothic style with soaring arches, fantastic acoustics and seats for about 1300 people. It has theatre style slanting from the back narthex down to the front of the altar. Carpet adorns the middle isle but the flooring under the pews is tile. So little carpet makes excellent singing acoustics but it also amplifies every little noise.

On this winter Sunday, there were more people than usual. Along with more people come the sneezing, coughing and hacking of winter colds and allergies. While service is going on, one heavy, young lady who is seated more than mid-way back has been continuously coughing. There are breaks in the sound, here and there, but it becomes obvious that it isn't going to stop anytime soon. As we reach the half way point in the morning service, it is now time for the Sermon. Everyone is quiet as the Minster steps up to the pulpit.

Moments into his sermon, the coughing begins once again. Slow and deep, she labors to get each one out. Then, a large burping sound followed by a flood of vomit that splatters onto the tile floor, echoing through the whole room. Instantly, several members immediately leave their seats, heading for the doors. The Minister is silent, holding his place and waiting to begin again. An aid rushes over to help. Another big burp and a second wave now floods the floor with a crash like a fire hose opening up to full capacity. A couple more people get up and move across the room to a new location. From the organ up in the choir loft, I have full view of everything that is happening. Finally, she is helped out of the room and the Minister continues after thanking the congregation for their patience. As the service continues, the sun glimmers through the stained glass window at just the perfect angle to illuminate the trail of liquid that is meandering down the slanted floor, under all of the pews and past the other congregants unseen. Once I see feet and liquid touch, I turn away.

I don't know how the others nearby held their composure but as soon as we finished singing the final hymn *"Are You Washed?"* everyone hurriedly left to go do just that.

Candle Trauma

Candles. Weddings wouldn't be complete without those beautiful little flickering sticks. Candles give everything an intimate glow and a warm beauty. Some weddings incorporate large candelabra's in mass on the altar and around the Sanctuary. Others opt for a more minimalistic approach, reducing the quantity down to only the customary Unity Candle Trio. Many or few, candles have a special place in weddings and other services. They also have a connection to danger.

A Wedding Coordinator once told me a story of a bride and groom making their way to the altar to light the single un-lit Unity Candle. Each of them lifted their individual candles, joined them together in the middle and then lowered them down slowly onto the unlit candle representing their unity. Then, each was to blow out their individual candle, leaving only their unity burning. Unfortunately, the bride forgot that she was wearing an extremely flammable organza veil. When she brought the flame towards her face, the veil burst into flames! Being such a fast burning fabric, the flame whooshed the fabric away instantly in a brilliant flash of light. Luckily, no one was injured. From that day forward, the wedding coordinator always warned each and every bride of the fire possibility and to keep their veil out of the way of the flame.

My own candle experience is far less flamboyant. Though not at a wedding, candles were involved. In the Advent Season, many churches have Advent Candle wreaths. During one morning service in 1997 the Advent Wreath candles on our altar were burning brightly. As soon as you burn a small portion of a new candle, it becomes obvious as to whether the candle was expensive or cheap. These were the cheapest. Midway through the sermon, the side of one of these fat candles gave way and the hot wax flowed out like lava from a volcano. Along with it, the wick was bending over like a young sapling. Still burning through the side of the candle the flame began to char the magnolia leaves of the wreath. Soon, there was a small fire dancing on the leaf.

Suddenly, one of my alert choir members jumped up, ran to the wreath and dumped his bottle of water on top. The minister abruptly stopped and everyone was startled and jumped from the commotion but his quick actions kept the candle from catching the whole wreath and the church on fire! Since then, we have a new yearly tradition. Whenever we all get together as a church family and decorate our Sanctuary and set out the wreath, someone always retells Ye Old Advent Candle Fire story once again and I smile, remembering the good old days of the 90's.

Kitty Kat Muff

In 2011, I finally exercised my contract option and gave my notice that I was no longer interested in playing for weddings anymore. When the minister at my church heard this, she quickly offered to pay me more money. As tempting as that was, I still decided I was finished with dealing with all of the normal and abnormal things that occur between the beginning of the wedding rehearsal to the end of the actual ceremony. Though I had been thinking about this for a long time, I finally made the decision definite following the last wedding I completed.

Over the years, couples usually have children to serve as ring-bearers. Sometimes, this means their own children or children of siblings or friends. They are so cute carrying the little pillow in front of them. Occasionally, the ring bearer is matched with the flower girl and they walk together, down the aisle as if they were the special couple. As like most children, they don't follow instructions well, take too long walking down the aisle or freak out completely, screaming and heading for a parent wherever they might be seated in the church. Each new wedding seemed to have younger and younger children trying desperately to carry that pillow and those flower petals, some barely walking. We had a policy outlined that no child below the age of two could be in the wedding party but people didn't pay any attention to it, frequently practically hand-walking babies down the aisle.

After seeing all of this, nothing prepared me for the last ring bearer named Prince. Prince was a large, seemingly docile Golden Retriever. He was very well behaved and a beautiful animal but should not have been included in the wedding. Strapped to his back was the normal pillow along with various ribbons and bows all in the matching color scheme of the people in the wedding. At the queue from the best man, Prince trotted down the aisle, alone, bringing the rings to the altar. At the rehearsal, everything was executed as planned and Prince made his theatrical debut to rave reviews of ohhhs and ahhhs. But at the actual wedding, just as Prince was starting his descent down the main isle, he spotted what he thought was a cat. Near the center isle was a guest with a white angora hand muff sitting on her lap. Prince bounded across the aisle and was on top of the lady in an instant. Shrieks ensued followed by screaming as Prince yanked the muff away and began flipping it wildly from side to side like a rope toy. The best man hurried to the aid of the lady but the muff was totally shredded. Thinking the best man was playing, Prince began to prance around the room, barking and looking for a way out. Eventually, he was captured and removed without further incident. When the tense service finally ended and I was finished, I decided that I really had seen everything and it was time now to change from playing weddings to playing funerals. At least at funerals, the pets of the deceased person are in mourning and will likely be less disruptive.

THE END

74

Andrew Whitenack is also author of

Mama's Family
The Unofficial Episode Viewing Guide

ANDDAR Publications

available at www.lulu.com